MW01490217

The Ultimate

Fondue Cookbook

Over 25 Cheese Fondue and Chocolate
Fondue Recipes

*Your Guide to Making the Best Fondue
Fountain Ever!*

By

Martha Stone

License Notes

No part of this Book can be reproduced in any form or by any means including print, electronic, scanning or photocopying unless prior permission is granted by the author.

All ideas, suggestions and guidelines mentioned here are written for informative purposes. While the author has taken every possible step to ensure accuracy, all readers are advised to follow information at their own risk. The author cannot be held responsible for personal and/or commercial damages in case of misinterpreting and misunderstanding any part of this Book.

About the author

Martha Stone is a chef and also cookbook writer. She was born and raised in Idaho where she spent most of her life growing up. Growing up in the country taught her how to appreciate and also use fresh ingredients in her cooking. This love for using the freshest ingredients turned into a passion for cooking. Martha loves to teach others how to cook and she loves every aspect of cooking from preparing the dish to smelling it cooking and sharing it with friends.

Martha eventually moved to California and met the love of her life. She settled down and has two children. She is a stay at home mom and involves her children in her cooking as much as possible. Martha decided to start writing cookbooks so that she could share her love for food and cooking with everyone else.

Table of Contents

Introduction

As impossible as it may seem, fondue seems to be making a comeback. Fondue itself has been transformed since the 1950's when it was solely made as a Swiss specialty to the international favorite it has come to be. Fondue itself is made during a variety of different holidays from New Year's Eve to Christmas.

Fondue's themselves can be made in a variety of different ways from savory cheese to sweet tasting dishes that will satisfy your strongest sweet tooth. Regardless of what kind of fondue dish you want to make, this book will help you do just that. Inside of this book you will find over 25 of the most delicious fondue recipes you will ever find as well as discover a few helpful tips to making your fondue dishes taste even more amazing.

So, without further ado, let's get cooking!

Delicious Fondue Recipes

Simple Cheese Fondue

This is a classic fondue recipe to serve up for any special occasion. For the tastiest results make sure that you use the best cheese you can find and pair this fondue dish with some pickled onions.

Makes: 8 Servings

Total Prep Time: 1 Hour and 5 Minutes

Ingredients:

- 24 Red Potatoes, Baby Variety
- 2 Quarts of Water
- 2 tsp. of Salt, For Taste
- 2 Tbsp. of Cornstarch
- 5 tsp. of Liqueur, Kirsch Variety
- 3 Cups of White Wine, Dry Variety
- 2 Cloves of Garlic, Minced
- 1 Pound of Cheese, Emmentaler Variety and Finely Shredded
- 1 Pound of Cheese, Gruyere Variety and Finely Shredded
- 1 tsp. of Nutmeg, Ground Variety
- 2 Loves of French Bread, Baguette Style and Cut into small Sized Pieces
- 1, 16 Ounce Jar of Onions, Pearl Variety, Pickled Variety and Drained
- 1, 12 Ounce Jar of Cornichons, Pickled Variety

Directions:

1. Place your potatoes into a large sized pot. Cover with enough water and season with a dash of salt. Set over medium heat and bring your water to a boil before reducing the heat to low. Cover and allow to cook for the next 20 minutes or until tender to the touch. Once tender, drain and set your potatoes aside for later use.

2. Next add your cornstarch and liqueur into a small sized bowl. Stir thoroughly until a paste begins to form. Set aside for later use.

3. Then combine your white wine and garlic in a large sized saucepan placed over medium heat. Bring this mixture to a simmer before whisking in your gruyere cheese and Emmentaler cheese. Allow to cook until fully melted.

4. Add in your cornstarch mixture and whisk thoroughly to combine. Add in your nutmeg and stir to combine.

5. Allow to cook for at least 8 to 10 minutes or until your mixture is thick in consistency.

6. Transfer your cheese mixture to a fondue pot and serve with your red potatoes and bread for dipping. Garnish with your onions and cornichons.

Beer and Cheese Fondue

Here is an unbelievable cheese fondue dish that I know you won't be able to get enough of. Serve this dish with some French bread for the tastiest results.

Makes: 6 Servings

Total Prep Time: 25 Minutes

Ingredients:

- 8 Ounces of Cheddar Cheese, Sharp Variety and Finely Shredded
- 8 Ounces of Swiss Cheese, Finely Shredded
- 2 Tbsp. of Flour, All Purpose Variety
- ½ tsp. of Salt, For Taste
- ¼ tsp. of Black Pepper, For Taste
- 1 Clove of Garlic, Cut into Halves

- 1, 12 Ounce Can of Beer, Your Favorite Kind
- Dash of Tabasco

Directions:

1. The first thing that you will want to do is combine your Swiss cheese, all-purpose flour, dash of salt, dash of pepper and cheddar cheese in a large sized bowl until evenly mixed.

2. Then take your garlic halves and rub them around the bottom and sides of the fondue pot you will be using.

3. Pour your beer into your fondue pot and bring to a simmer over low to medium heat. This should take at least 5 minutes.

4. Slowly add in your cheese mixture and cook for the next 10 to 15 minutes or until fully melted.

5. Add in your Tabasco and stir to combine. Serve whenever you are ready and enjoy.

Healthy Creamy Veggie Fondue

Here is a classic and absolutely delicious twist on a classic cheese fondue recipe that I know you are going to love. Feel free to add whatever kind of cheeses and veggies you wish to this dish to make it truly unique.

Makes: 32 Servings

Total Prep Time: 35 Minutes

Ingredients:

- ¼ Cup of Milk, Whole
- ¼ Cup of White Wine, Your Favorite Kind
- 1, 8 Ounces of Cheddar Cheese, Finely Shredded
- 1, 8 Ounce Pack of Monterey Jack Cheese, Finely Shredded
- 1, 8 Ounce Pack of Cream Cheese, Soft

- ¼ Cup of Green Onions, Finely Chopped
- ¼ Cup of Spinach, Frozen, Thawed, Drained and Roughly Chopped
- 1 tsp. of Mustard, Dry and Ground
- 1 tsp. of Cayenne Pepper, Ground
- 1 tsp. of Garlic, Powdered Variety
- 1 tsp. of Black Pepper, For Taste

Directions:

1. Use a medium sized saucepan and set over medium heat. Add in your milk, wine, cheddar cheese, shredded Monterey jack cheese and soft cream cheese. Stir thoroughly to combine and cook for the next 10 minutes, making sure to stir frequently.

2. Then add in your green onions, frozen Spinach, dried mustard, dash of cayenne pepper, powdered garlic and dash of black pepper. Continue to cook for the next 10 minutes or until your ingredients are thoroughly blended.

3. Transfer this mixture to a fondue pot that you are using and serve whenever you are ready.

Tasty Bread Pot Fondue

This is a delicious appetizer that I know you are going to love to enjoy over and over again. Packed with a variety of different flavors, I know you won't be able to get enough of it.

Makes: 32 Servings

Total Prep Time: 1 Hour and 30 Minutes

Ingredients:

- 1, 1 Pound Loaf of Bread, Round Variety
- 1, 8 Ounce Pack of Cheddar Cheese, Finely Shredded
- 2, 3 Ounce Packs of Cream Cheese, Soft
- 1 ½ Cups of Sour Cream
- 1 Cup of Ham, Fully Cooked and Finely Diced
- ½ Cup of Green Onions, Finely Chopped
- 1, 4 Ounce Can of Green Chile Peppers, Finely Diced
- 1 tsp. of Worcestershire Sauce
- 2 Tbsp. of Oil, Vegetable Variety
- 1 Tbsp. of Butter, Fully Melted

Directions:

1. The first thing that you will want to do is preheat your oven to 350 degrees.

2. While your oven is heating up cut a circle into the top of your bread. Remove the top and hallow out the inside of your loaf, making sure to reserve the bread that you have removed for dipping later on.

3. Then use a medium sized bowl and add in your soft cream cheese, shredded Cheddar cheese, cooked ham, chopped green onions, sour cream, chopped green peppers and Worcestershire sauce. Stir thoroughly to combine.

4. Spoon this mixture into your bread bowl and replace the top. Wrap your loaf in some aluminum foil and place onto a greased large sized baking sheet.

5. Place into your oven to bake for the next hour or until your cheese is fully melted.

6. While your bread is baking, cut up your reserved bread into small sized pieces. Toss the pieces with some oil and butter.

7. Place onto a separate large sized baking sheet and place into your oven to toast for the next 10 to 15 minutes or until golden brown in color.

8. Remove and serve right away.

Best Three Cheese Fondue

With this delicious three cheese fondue, your friends and family won't want to use simple and basic cheese fondue again. It is tangy in flavor and makes for the most delicious meal you will ever have.

Makes: 24 Servings

Total Prep Time: 30 Minutes

Ingredients:

- 1 Cup of White Wine, Your Favorite Kind
- 1 Tbsp. of Butter, Soft
- 1 Tbsp. of Flour, All Purpose Variety
- 7 Ounces of Cheese, Gruyere Variety and Cut into Cubes

- 7 Ounces of Cheddar Cheese, Sharp Variety and Cut into Small Sized Cubes
- 7 Ounces of Cheese, Emmentaler Variety and Cut into Cubes

Directions:

1. The first thing that you will want to do is bring your white wine to a boil in a small sized saucepan.

2. Then melt your butter in a medium sized saucepan placed over low to medium heat. Once melted whisk in your flour and cook for the next 5 minutes, making sure to whisk frequently during this time.

3. After this time add in your wine and whisk until smooth in consistency.

4. Slowly add in your remaining Gruyere, Cheddar and Emmentaler cheeses, making sure to stir thoroughly until completely melted.

5. Transfer this mixture to a fondue pot that you are using and serve whenever you are ready.

Brie Cheese Fondue

If you are a huge fan of brie cheese, then I know you are going to love this fondue dish. It is the best fondue dish to make whenever you are looking to make something special for that special someone in your life.

Makes: 4 Servings

Total Prep Time: 30 Minutes

Ingredients:

- 2 Cloves of Garlic, Finely Crushed
- 1 Cup of White Wine, Dried Variety
- ¼ Cup of Sherry

- 1 Pound of Brie Cheese, Rind Removed and Cut into Cubes
- 1 Tbsp. of Cornstarch
- Dash of Nutmeg, Freshly Grated
- Dash of Salt and Pepper, For Taste

Directions:

1. The first thing that you will want to do is rub your garlic over the inside and bottom of your fondue pot, making sure to leave the crushed pieces in your fondue pot.

2. Next add your white wine and sherry to a small sized pot and set over low to medium heat.

3. Add in your brie cheese in your cornstarch into a small sized bowl. Toss thoroughly to coat.

4. Once your wine is hot to the touch, add in your coated cheese. Cook until your cheese is fully melted.

5. Remove from heat and add in a dash of nutmeg, dash of salt and dash of pepper. Stir your mixture until your cheese is smooth in consistency.

6. Transfer this mixture to a fondue pot that you are using and serve whenever you are ready.

Savory Irish Stout Fondue

Here is yet another fondue dish that you are going to fall in love with. Made with your favorite kind of beer and three types of cheese, it is one type of cheese that you won't be able to get enough of. For the tastiest results serve this fondue with your favorite bread, veggies and types of meat.

Makes: 8 Servings

Total Prep Time: 25 Minutes

Ingredients:

- 1 1/8 Cups of Cheddar Cheese, Extra Sharp Variety, White in Color and Finely Shredded
- 1 1/8 Cups of Swiss Cheese, Finely Shredded
- 2 Tbsp. of Parmesan Cheese, Freshly Shredded
- 1 ½ Tbsp. of Cornstarch

- 1/2, 12 Ounce Can of Stout Beer, Irish Variety
- 1 Tbsp. of Steak Sauce, Your Favorite Kind
- 1 tsp. of Worcestershire Sauce
- 1 tsp. of Garlic, Powdered Variety
- ½ tsp. of Hot Sauce, Your Favorite Kind
- ¼ tsp. of Mustard, Dry and Ground Variety
- Dash of Black Pepper, For Taste

Directions:

1. Add your white cheese, Swiss cheese, grated Parmesan cheese and cornstarch into a small sized bowl. Stir thoroughly to combine and set aside for later use.

2. Add your beer, favorite steak sauce, Worcestershire sauce, powdered garlic, favorite hot sauce and powdered mustard into your fondue pot.

3. Set your fondue pot over medium heat and stir thoroughly to combine.

4. Add in your cheese mixture slowly into your pot and stir thoroughly until your cheese is fully melted and your cheese is smooth in consistency.

5. Remove from heat and serve whenever you are ready.

Shrimp Packed Fondue

If you are a huge fan of shrimp, then this is one fondue dish that you are going to fall in love with. It is rich in taste, creamy in consistency and packed full of a taste you will want to enjoy over and over again.

Makes: 7 Servings

Total Prep Time: 15 Minutes

Ingredients:

- 1, 16 Ounce Container of Sour Cream
- 1, 8 Ounce Pack of Cream Cheese, Soft
- 1, 10.75 Can of Cream of Shrimp Soup
- Dash of Worcestershire Sauce
- Dash of Salt, Garlic Variety

Directions:

1. The first thing that you will want to do is add in your sour cream, soft cream cheese, cream of shrimp soup, dash of garlic salt and Worcestershire sauce into a medium sized pot.

2. Set over medium heat and cook until fully melted or until your mixture is creamy in consistency.

3. Transfer this mixture to a fondue pot that you are using and serve whenever you are ready.

Savory Parmesan Fondue

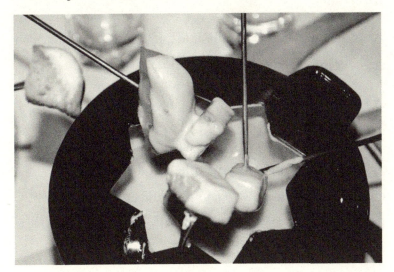

This is a warm and creamy fondue that is mild in taste, making it perfect for those who are picky eaters in your household. Serve this dish with your favorite kind of bread, veggies or meat for the tastiest results.

Makes: 14 Servings

Total Prep Time: 10 Minutes

Ingredients:

- 1, 8 Ounce Pack of Neufchatel Cheese
- 1 Cup of Milk, Whole
- ¾ Cup of Parmesan Cheese, Freshly Grated
- ½ tsp. of Salt, Garlic Variety
- 1 Loaf of Bread, Small in Size, French Variety and Cut into Small Sized Cubes

Directions:

1. Add your cheese and milk into a medium sized saucepan set over low to meat heat.

2. Cook until your cheese is fully melted. This should take at least 2 to 3 minutes.

3. Then add in your dash of garlic salt and parmesan cheese. Stir thoroughly to combine and continue to cook until your parmesan cheese is fully melted. This should take at least 2 to 3 minutes.

4. Transfer this mixture to a fondue pot that you are using and serve whenever you are ready with your bread cubes.

Simple Pizza Fondue

Here is yet another creative and unique fondue dish that I know even the pickiest of eaters will want you to make over and over again. Both kids and adults will fall in love with it.

Makes: 6 Servings

Total Prep Time: 35 Minutes

Ingredients:

- 1, 26 Ounce Jar of Spaghetti Sauce, Meatless Variety
- 1, 8 Ounce Pack of Mozzarella Cheese, Finely Shredded
- ¼ Cup of Parmesan Cheese, Freshly Grated
- 2 tsp. of Oregano, Dried
- 1 tsp. of Onion, Dried and Minced
- ¼ tsp. of Salt, Garlic Variety
- 1, 16 Ounce Loaf of French Bread, Cut into Small Sized Cubes

Directions:

1. Add your meatless spaghetti sauce, mozzarella cheese, grated parmesan cheese, dried oregano, dried onion and dash of garlic salt into a medium sized fondue pot. Stir thoroughly to combine.

2. Place your fondue over medium heat, making sure to stir thoroughly.

3. Cook until your cheese fully melts. Remove from heat.

4. Transfer this mixture to a fondue pot that you are using and serve whenever you are ready with your bread. Enjoy.

Tequila Fondue

Here is a tasty fondue dish that you can make whenever you want to impress your friends and family. Made with a touch of tequila, cream and avocado. For the tastiest results serve this dish with some shrimp or bread for dipping.

Makes: 8 Servings

Total Prep Time: 40 Minutes

Ingredients:

- 6 Tbsp. of Butter, Soft
- 1 Clove of Garlic, Minced
- 2 Onions, Small in Size and Finely Chopped
- 2 Tbsp. of Flour, All Purpose Variety
- 1 Avocado, Fresh, Peeled and Pitted
- ½ Cup of Cream, Whipping Variety
- 1 Cup of Milk, Whole
- 3 Tbsp. of Lemon Juice, Fresh
- 2 Tbsp. of Tequila, Your Favorite Kind
- ½ Cup of Cotija Cheese, Finely Crumbled
- Dash of Salt and Pepper, For Taste

Directions:

1. First melt your butter in a large sized skillet placed over medium heat. Once your butter is fully melted add in your onions and cook until tender to the touch.

2. Then add in your garlic and cook for at least a minute.

3. After this time add in your flour and whisk thoroughly until smooth in consistency and cook until brown in color. Remove from heat and set aside for later use.

4. Next preheat your oven to 350 degrees.

5. While your oven is heating up add your avocado into a blender. Add in your milk, whipping cream and fresh lemon juice. Season with a dash of salt and pepper.

6. Blend on the highest setting until smooth in consistency.

7. Pour your mixture into a medium sized generously greased baking dish. Add in your onion and garlic mixture. Stir thoroughly to combine.

8. Place into your oven to bake for the next 20 minutes or until thick in consistency.

9. After this time add in your tequila and cheese. Stir thoroughly to combine.

10. Place into your oven to bake for the next 5 minutes or until your cheese is fully melted.

11. Transfer this mixture to a fondue pot that you are using and serve whenever you are ready.

Healthy Cheese and Tomato Fondue

Here is a fondue recipe that is easy to make and tastes absolutely amazing. For the tastiest results I highly recommend serving this dish with your favorite sliced baguettes.

Makes: 24 Servings

Total Prep Time: 40 Minutes

Ingredients:

- 2 Tbsp. of Butter, Soft
- 2 Cloves of Garlic, Pressed
- ½ tsp. of Onion, Minced
- 3 Tomatoes, Small in Size, Seeded and Finely Chopped
- 1 ½ Cups of White Wine, Dried
- 1 Pound of Cheese, Gruyere Variety and Finely Shredded
- ½ Pound of Swiss Cheese, Finely Shredded

Directions:

1. Using a large sized fondue pot, place it over medium heat and add in your butter. Cook until fully melted before adding in your garlic and onions. Cook until your vegetables are tender to the touch.

2. Add in your tomatoes and continue to cook for an additional 3 minutes.

3. Pour in your wine and continue to stir until mixture reaches a boil.

5. After this time remove from heat and add in Gruyere and Swiss cheese. Stir thoroughly until fully melted. Serve whenever you are ready and enjoy.

Healthy Tomato, Gouda Cheese and Basil Fondue

If you have been looking for a different and unique fondue recipe to enjoy, then this is the perfect dish for you to enjoy. It is made with healthy ingredients and makes for a tasty fondue dish that you don't have to feel guilty about enjoying.

Makes: 6 Servings

Total Prep Time: 15 Minutes

Ingredients:

- 8 Ounces of gouda Cheese, Cut into Small Sized Pieces
- 1/3 Cup of Tomato, Fresh and Finely Diced
- 1 Tbsp. of Basil, Fresh and Roughly Chopped
- 1 Baguette, French Variety, Sliced and Lightly Toasted

Directions:

1. Add your Gouda cheese into a small sized microwave safe bowl.

2. Place your bowl into your oven to cook for the next minute, making sure to check it every 30 seconds.

3. Make sure to cook until it is fully melted

4. Add in your tomato and basil. Stir thoroughly to combine.

5. Transfer this mixture to a fondue pot that you are using and serve whenever you are ready with your bread slices. Enjoy.

Soft Cream Cheese Fondue

This is one fondue dish that you can make if you have a few cream cheese lovers in your household. Made with a dash of nutmeg and sherry helps make this fondue dish incredibly delicious.

Makes: 4 Servings

Total Prep Time: 15 Minutes

Ingredients:

- 2, 8 Ounce Packs of Cream Cheese, Soft and Cut into Small Sized Cubes
- 1 ¾ Cups of Milk, Whole
- 1 Tbsp. of Sherry, Dry Variety
- 2 tsp. of Mustard, Powdered Variety
- 1 tsp. of Salt, Garlic Variety
- Dash of Black Pepper, For Taste
- Dash of Nutmeg, Ground Variety

Directions:

1. Add your cream cheese and whole milk into a large sized saucepan. Place over medium heat and cook until your cheese is completely melted. This should take at least 5 to 7 minutes.

2. After this time add in your ground nutmeg, dash of pepper, dried sherry, powdered mustard and garlic salt. Stir thoroughly to combine.

3. Continue to cook until your cream cheese is completely melted. This should take at least 3 minutes.

4. Transfer this mixture to a fondue pot that you are using and serve whenever you are ready.

Decadent Chocolate and Caramel Fondue

If you are a huge fan of chocolate and caramel, then this is one fondue recipe that you are going to fall in love with. Feel free to use your favorite kind of chocolate for this dish for the tastiest results.

Makes: 4 Servings

Total Prep Time: 40 Minutes

Ingredients:

- 1, 14 Ounce Pack of Caramels
- 1, 5 Ounce Can of Milk, Evaporated Variety
- ½ Cup of Chocolate, Semi-Sweet Variety
- ½ tsp. of Vanilla, Pure

Directions:

1. The first thing that you will want to do is use a large sized bowl and add in your remaining ingredients.

2. Place into a baking dish and place into your oven to bake for the next 350 degrees for the next 30 minutes or until smooth in consistency.

3. Remove and stir thoroughly until smooth in consistency.

4. Transfer this mixture to a fondue pot that you are using and serve whenever you are ready. Enjoy.

Savory Pumpkin Fondue

Here is another great fondue recipe to make whenever pumpkin seems to be the only thing the world can think about. It is different in taste and makes it perfect to serve up during the holiday season.

Makes: 12 to 18 Servings

Total Prep Time: 25 Minutes

Ingredients for Your Fondue:

- 1 Clove of Garlic, Smashed
- 1 ¾ Cup of Apple Cider, Hard Variety
- ¾ Cup of Pumpkin Puree, Fresh
- ¼ tsp. of Mustard, Powdered Variety
- ¼ tsp. of Cayenne Pepper
- ¼ tsp. of Your Mixed Spiced (See Below)
- ½ tsp. of Sea Salt, For Taste
- 2 Tbsp. of Flour, All Purpose Variety
- ½ Cup of Cheddar Cheese, Freshly Grated
- ¼ Cup of Gruyere Cheese, Freshly Grated
- 3 Ounces of Brie Cheese, Rind Remove
- 1 tsp. of Lemon Juice, Fresh

Ingredients for Your Mixed Spices:

- 1 Tbsp. of Cinnamon, Ground Variety
- ½ tsp. of Allspice, Dried
- ¼ tsp. of Nutmeg
- ¼ tsp. of Cloves
- 1/8 tsp. of Ginger, Ground

Directions:

1. The first thing that you will want to do is set a medium sized saucepan over medium heat.

2. Once your saucepan is hot enough add in your garlic, hard apple cider, pumpkin puree, powdered mustard, cayenne pepper, your mixed spices and dash of sea salt. Stir thoroughly to combine.

3. Bring this mixture to a boil. Once boiling reduce the heat to low.

4. While your mixture is simmering mix together your flour, cheddar cheese, brie cheese and gruyere cheese in a small sized bowl, making sure to toss thoroughly to coat.

5. Add your cheese to your pumpkin mixture, making sure to whisk thoroughly until fully melted.

6. Add in your fresh lemon juice. Stir to combine and remove from heat.

7. Transfer this mixture to a fondue pot that you are using and serve whenever you are ready with some apples, vegetables or bread for the tastiest results.

Wild Mushroom and Brie Fondue

If you are looking for something on the hearty and wild side, then this is the perfect fondue recipe for you to make. Just consisting of a few ingredients, no fondue dish is as easy to make as this one.

Makes: 5 Servings

Total Prep Time: 40 Minutes

Ingredients:

- 1 Cup of Water, Warm
- 1 Ounce of Mushrooms, Porcini Variety and Dried
- 2 Tbsp. of Butter, Soft
- 8 Ounces of Mushrooms, Shiitake Variety and Fresh
- 2 Tbsp. of Shallots, Finely Chopped
- 1 Pound of Brie Cheese, Rind Trimmed and Cut into Small Sized Cubes
- 2 Tbsp. of Cornstarch
- Some Asparagus, Fresh and for Serving
- 1 Piece of Bread, French Variety and Lightly Toasted
- 1 Piece of Chicken, Fully Cooked and for Serving

Directions:

1. First bring at least one cup of water to a boil in a small sized saucepan. Once your water is boiling add in your porcini mushrooms. Remove from heat and allow to sit in your water for the next 20 minutes or until your mushrooms are soft to the touch. Once soft drain and finely chop your mushrooms.

2. Next melt your butter in a large sized saucepan over medium heat. Once your butter is melted add in your shiitake mushrooms and cook until tender to the touch. This should take at least 3 minutes.

3. After this time add in your shallots and cook for an additional minute.

4. Then add in your porcini mushrooms along with some cooking liquid. Increase the heat to high and allow to simmer for the next 3 minutes or until the liquid fully evaporates.

5. While your mixture is simmering add your brie cheese and cornstarch into a large sized bowl. Toss thoroughly to combine.

6. Add your wine into your mushroom mixture and bring to a simmer over medium heat.

7. Add your cheese to your mushroom mixture and continuously whisk until your mixture is smooth in consistency.

8. Season with a dash of salt and pepper.

9. Transfer this mixture to a fondue pot that you are using and serve whenever you are ready with some bread, chicken and asparagus for the tastiest results.

Simple Three Ingredient Caramel Fondue

If you are looking for a relatively simple fondue dish to prepare, it really doesn't get any easier than this dish. Made by using only three ingredients, you can make this fondue dish on the stovetop or in your microwave.

Makes: 6 Servings

Total Prep Time: 10 Minutes

Ingredients:

- 25 Caramels, Soft and Unwrapped
- 1/3 Cup of Cream, Heavy Variety
- 1/3 Cup of Marshmallows, Miniature Variety
- ½ tsp. of Sea Salt, For Taste and Optional
- Some Apples, Cut into Pieces and for Serving
- Some Bananas, Thinly Sliced and for Serving

Directions:

1. First add your caramels and cream into a large sized microwave safe bowl.

2. Place into your microwave to cook on the highest setting for the next 2 to 3 minutes.

3. After this time stir thoroughly until smooth in consistency. Return to your microwave to cook for an additional minute or two if you need to.

4. Add in your marshmallows and salt if you are using it. Stir thoroughly until your marshmallows melt completely.

5. Transfer this mixture to a fondue pot that you are using and serve whenever you are ready with your apples and bananas.

Savory Beef and Chicken Fondue

With this delicious fondue recipe, you will never want to enjoy beef or chicken again without it. It is easy to make and will satisfy every picky eater in your household.

Makes: 8 Servings

Total Prep Time: 2 Hours and 30 Minutes

Ingredients for Your Creamy Cucumber Sauce:

- 2, 3 Ounce Packs of Cream Cheese, Soft
- 2 Cups of Sour Cream
- ¼ Cup of Milk, Whole
- 1 Cup of Cucumber, Peeled and Finely Chopped
- 2 Tbsp. of Onion, Finely Chopped
- ½ tsp. of Salt, For Taste

Ingredients for Your Fondue:

- 1 Pound of Sirloin Steak, Beef Variety
- 1 Pound of Chicken Breasts, Boneless and Skinless Variety
- Some Lettuce, Fresh
- 1, 8 Ounce Pack of Mushrooms, White in Color, Fresh and Whole
- 2 Bell Peppers, Medium in Size and Cut into Small Sized Pieces
- 2 Carrots, Fresh, Medium in Size and Cut into Small Sized Pieces
- 2 Cups of Broccoli, Cut into Florets and Fresh
- 4, 14 Ounce Cans of Chicken Broth, Homemade Preferable
- 2, 14 Ounce Cans of Beef Broth, Homemade Preferable
- 4 Cloves of Garlic, Peeled
- 4 tsp. of Parsley Flakes, Dried
- 2 tsp. of Thyme Leaves, Dried
- ½ tsp. of Salt, For Taste
- ½ tsp. of Pepper, For Taste

Directions:

1. The first thing that you will want to do is make your creamy cucumber sauce. To do this use a medium sized bowl and beat your cream cheese with an electric mixer until smooth in consistency.

2. Add in your remaining cucumber sauce ingredients and stir to thoroughly combine.

3. Cover with some plastic wrap and place into your fridge to chill for the next 2 hours.

4. Place your chicken and steak onto a plated lined with your fresh lettuce leaves. Cover and place into your fridge to sit until you are ready.

5. Divide up your broth between two fondue pots. Add in half of your garlic, dried thyme, parsley flakes and dash of salt and pepper into each pot. Heat until piping hot.

6. Arrange your platter with your meat around your fondue pots and serve whenever you are ready.

Sweet Tasting Snickers Fondue

Here is a fondue dish that is rich in taste, creamy in consistency and absolutely delicious that nobody in your home will be able to turn it away. On top of that it is very easy to make and you can have it on your table in a matter of minutes.

Makes: 4 Servings

Total Prep Time: 15 Minutes

Ingredients:

- 2 Snicker Bars, Almond Variety
- 1 Snickers Bar, Regular
- 1 Cup of Chocolate Chips, Milk Variety
- 7 Ounces of Marshmallow Crème
- ¾ Cup of Cream, Heavy Whipping Variety

Directions:

1. The first thing that you will want to do is heat up your fondue pot over low to medium heat.

2. While your fondue pot is heating up break your snickers bars into small sized pieces.

3. Add your broken up snickers bars into your fondue pot along with your remaining ingredients and stir thoroughly to combine.

4. Cook until your chocolate melts completely and your cream in piping hot. Stir thoroughly as it cooks.

5. Reduce the heat to low and serve with your favorite dipping ingredients. Enjoy.

Savory Pesto Fondue

Looking for an Italian inspired fondue dish? Then this is the perfect dish for you to make. For the tastiest results I highly recommend serving this dish with some fresh Italian bread or even pasta.

Makes: 4 Servings

Total Prep Time: 15 Minutes

Ingredients:

- 3 Cups of Mozzarella Cheese, Finely Shredded
- 1 Cup of Parmesan Cheese, Finely Shredded
- 1 ½ Cups of White Wine, Dry Variety
- 2 Tbsp. of Cornstarch
- 3 Cloves of Garlic, Minced
- ½ Cup of Basil Leaves, Fresh and Roughly Torn

- ¼ Cup of Almonds, Lightly Toasted
- Dash of Black Pepper, For Taste

Directions:

1. Place your almonds, torn basil and minced garlic into a food processor. Blend on the highest setting until evenly chopped.

2. Then add in at least ¼ cup of your wine and blend again until smooth in consistency. Remove and set aside for later use.

3. Next use a large sized saucepan and add in your freshly made pesto mixture. Add in your remaining white wine and bring to a low boil.

4. Use a large sized bowl and add in your mozzarella and parmesan cheese along with your cornstarch. Stir thoroughly to combine and slowly add into your pesto and wine mixture, making sure to stir thoroughly as you do so.

5. Season with a dash of salt and pepper.

6. Transfer this mixture to a fondue pot that you are using and serve whenever you are ready.

Irish Whisky Cheddar Fondue

If you are looking for a fondue dish that you can make to satisfy your significant other, then this is the perfect dish for you to make. This is a great dish to make for a romantic evening or whenever you want to spoil that special someone in your life.

Makes: 6 Servings

Total Prep Time: 25 Minutes

Ingredients:

- 1 Clove of Garlic, Cut into Halves
- 1 Cup of White Wine, Dry Variety
- 1 ½ Pound of Cheddar Cheese, Irish Variety and Freshly Grated
- 1 ½ Tbsp. of Cornstarch
- 2 Tbsp. of Whiskey, Irish Variety
- Dash of Sea Salt, For Taste
- Dash of Black Pepper, For Taste

Directions:

1. The first thing that you will want to do is rub your garlic all of the sides of a large sized fondue pot. Then place over medium to high heat.

2. Add in your wine and bring to a simmer.

3. While your wine is simmer toss your cheese with your cornstarch until evenly mixed. Gently add to your wine.

4. Stir thoroughly until your cheese melts completely.

5. Once melted add in your whiskey and continue to cook for the next 1 to 2 minutes or until your mixture is bubbling.

6. Season with a dash of salt and pepper.

7. Transfer this mixture to a fondue pot that you are using and serve whenever you are ready.

Mexican Style Fondue

With only a handful of ingredients and very little time in regards to prep work, then this is one festive fondue dish that you will want to enjoy over and over again. I know you will fall in love with it, especially if you are looking for something on the Hispanic side.

Makes: 18 Servings

Total Prep Time: 1 Hour and 45 Minutes

Ingredients:

- 1, 14.75 Ounce Can of Corn, Cream Style
- 1, 14.5 Ounce Can of Tomatoes, Finely Diced and Drained
- 3 Tbsp. of Green Chilies, Finely Chopped
- 1 tsp. of Chili, Powdered Variety
- 1, 16 Ounce Pack of Velveeta Cheese and Cut into Cubes
- Some Cubes of Bread, French Variety and for Dipping

Directions:

1. Use a small sized bowl and add in your cream corn, diced tomatoes, powdered chili and green chilies.

2. Add in your cheese and stir thoroughly to combine.

3. Pour this mixture into a medium sized greased slow cooker.

4. Cover and cook on the highest setting for the next 1 ½ hours, making sure to stir thoroughly every 30 minutes or until your cheese is fully melted.

5. After this time transfer this mixture to a fondue pot that you are using and serve with your French bread cubes. Enjoy.

Classic Chocolate Fondue

If you have been looking for a classic chocolate fondue dish that you can make whenever you are craving it, then this is the perfect dish for you to make. Feel free to dip whatever kind of ingredients you want into this dish. Regardless, you are going to love it.

Makes: 4 Servings

Total Prep Time: 20 Minutes

Ingredients:

- 8 Ounces of Chocolate Chips, Milk Variety
- 2 Tbsp. of Cream, Heavy Whipping Variety
- 2 Tbsp. of Peanut Butter, Chunky Variety

Directions:

1. First combine your chocolate chips and heavy cream in a large sized bowl. Stir to combine and pour into a small sized saucepan.

2. Set over low heat and allow to cook until the chocolate chips melt completely. Make sure that you stir frequently as it does this.

3. Add in your peanut butter and stir to combine or until smooth in consistency.

4. Cook for another minutes before transferring this mixture to a fondue pot that you are using and serve whenever you are ready.

Creamy Caramelized Shallot and Gruyere Cheese Fondue

This is a great dish to make during the Christmas holidays while you are setting up the family Christmas tree. Serve with delicious and fresh sourdough bread to fill your house with moans of delight from all those who try a bite.

Makes: 8 Servings

Total Prep Time: 35 Minutes

- Ingredients:
- 1 Tbsp. of Butter, Soft
- 6 Ounces of Shallots, Sliced Thinly
- 1 tsp. of Sugar, White in Color
- 1 tsp. of Salt, For Taste
- 14 Ounces of Gruyere Cheese, Freshly Grated
- 2 Tbsp. of Flour, All Purpose Variety
- 1 ½ Cups of White Wine, Dry Variety
- Dash of Nutmeg, Ground
- 1 Clove of Garlic, Minced
- 2 Tbsp. of Brandy, Apple Variety
- Dash of Black Pepper, For Taste

Directions:

1. First melt your butter in a medium sized saucepan placed over medium heat. Once your butter is melted add in your shallots and cook them for the next 2 minutes.

2. Then add in your sugar and dash of salt. Continue to cook while stirring occasionally for the next 15 minutes.

3. Add your grated cheese to a large sized bowl and add in your flour. Toss to thoroughly combine.

4. Add your white wine to your cooked shallots and allow to come to a boil for at least one minute.

5. Slowly whisk in your cheese and continue to cook until fully melted.

6. Once melted add in your nutmeg, minced garlic, apple brandy and dash of pepper. Stir to combine and remove from heat.

7. Transfer this mixture to a fondue pot that you are using and serve whenever you are ready.

Mouthwatering S'mores Fondue

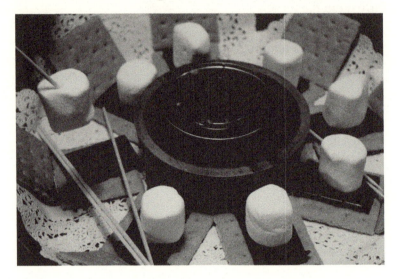

If you are a huge fan of classic s'mores, then this is one fondue recipe I know you are going to want to make 0ver and over again. This is the perfect dish to make for little mouths in your house as a special treat for everybody to enjoy.

Makes: 4 Servings

Total Prep Time: 12 Minutes

Ingredients:

- ½ to ¾ Cup of Half and Half
- Dash of Salt, For Taste and Optional
- 5 to 6 Chocolate Bars, Milk Variety and Broken into Small Sized Pieces
- Some Marshmallows, To Cover Your Chocolate

- Some Graham Crackers, For Dipping
- Some Strawberries, Fresh and for Dipping

Directions:

1. Use a medium sized microwave safe bowl and add in your half and half and salt, if you are using it.

2. Place into your microwave to cook on the highest setting for the next 1 to 2 minutes. Make sure your mixture does not boil.

3. Add in your chocolate pieces and allow to sit for at least one minute. After this time whisk thoroughly until smooth in consistency.

4. Pour your chocolate mixture into your fondue pot and cover with your marshmallows.

5. Place under a broiler for the next 5 minutes or until your marshmallows are brown in color.

6. Remove and serve immediately with your graham crackers and strawberries. Enjoy!

Conclusion

Well, there you have it!

Hopefully by the end of this book you have been able to satisfy all of your fondue cravings. I hope that by the end of this book you have learned not only how to make the most delicious fondue recipes you have ever tasted, but have also learned what you need in order to make these dishes even more delicious.

So, what is the next step for you?

The next step for you to take is to begin making all of the fondue recipes you have found in this book. Once you have done that I highly recommend trying to make your own fondue recipes from scratch, using only the ingredients that you love and that your entire family loves.

Don't worry! I have complete faith in you!

Good luck!

Author's Afterthoughts

Thank you for reading my book. Your feedback is important to us. It would be greatly appreciated if you could please take a moment to *REVIEW* this book on Amazon so that we could make our next version better

Thanks!

Martha Stone

martha@168publishing.com

Made in the USA
Coppell, TX
04 January 2022